GW00726093

RECOVERING THE WORD

The need for expository preaching today

James Philip

Fellowship of Word and Spirit

Further copies of *Orthos* and information about the Fellowship may be obtained from:
Fellowship of Word and Spirit, 7 The Green, Hartford, Northwich, Cheshire CW8 1QA.

Printed in Great Britain by
Tyndale Press (Lowestoft) Ltd., Wollaston Road, Lowestoft, Suffolk NR32 2PD.

ISBN 1 874694 00 1

RECOVERING THE WORD
The need for expository preaching today

Dr Martin Luther King, the American Civil Rights leader and Nobel Peace Prize winner, stirred the hearts of countless people all over the world by his moving and famous speech which began with the words 'I have a dream ...'. Lesser men may also have visions and dreams, and I have one also. I want to make a case for expository preaching. My conviction — and this has been the basis on which my own ministry has been built over the last forty years — is that unless there is a recovery, a rehabilitation indeed, of the biblical doctrine of preaching, the process of decay within the life of the church is likely to continue and accelerate.

Introduction

The first thing I think it is necessary to do is to set this theme in some kind of historical perspective. By way of introduction, perhaps a brief, autobiographical note at the outset will not be out of order. The first eight years of my ministry (following an eighteen-month probationary assistantship in Glasgow) were spent in the north-east of Scotland in a little fishing community with an evangelical, even evangelistic, tradition, and I followed a man who had ministered there for seventeen years without seeing all that much response. My years were years of reaping, and we saw 'great days of the Son of Man', with the Spirit of God working in many lives in what I suppose was as near to the classical manifestations of revival as has been seen in the post-war years, with an awesome sense of eternity brooding over the place, and people being wrought upon by the Spirit with startling suddenness and sometimes without even being in church. But they were also days in which I learned the dangers of mere evangelistic zeal running to seed, and God laid on my heart the need for a teaching ministry in depth that would have as its aim the building up of Christian character.

When I was called to Edinburgh more than thirty-one years ago, I felt that my task was to expound the Scriptures systematically, book by book. What I felt God was saying to me was 'Go there, preach my Word, and establish my Word in that place!' Full stop! That was all. So I did not feel free to take any particular line, nor impose any particular pattern on the work. My task and my remit were to expound the Scriptures. This I have sought, and have been content, to do.

I realize now, as perhaps I could not have done then, that such an attitude and such a practice make certain definite assumptions about the nature of preaching itself, and flow from a certain doctrine of preaching. It was hardly surprising, therefore — and this brings me to the historical perspective I have referred to — that when my Kirk Session generously urged upon me a six-month sabbatical period, I took the opportunity of engaging in a study of the history of preaching. One of the things which more immediately sparked off this study was the reading of the biography of a well-known Scottish preacher, J.P. Struthers of Greenock. Struthers maintained a friendship and correspondence over many years with the great James Denney of Trinity College, Glasgow. It was the reading of some of the letters that passed between them, particularly Struthers' requests to Denney to send him some of his sermons and 'a text to preach on next Sunday', that led to the realization that so much of the preaching of those days was 'textual' preaching rather than continuous exposition. Moreover, this was in fact the pattern followed by many of the prominent figures of the nineteenth century — McCheyne, the Bonars, Spurgeon — and that a large part of the preaching of the eighteenth century and much of that of the seventeenth seems to have been of this sort, in sharp contrast to Calvin and the Reformers, who pursued a policy of systematic exposition of the Scriptures, preaching through the entire Bible, book by book, in the space of ten years.

It became quickly evident to me, after even a cursory, preliminary consideration of this subject, that nothing less than an examination of the whole history of preaching from its earliest origins, however condensed, could suffice to do any kind of justice to the subject. This I sought to do, and although it cannot be my concern to go into this in detail now, it will suffice to say that the preaching patterns that developed in the post-Reformation era in the seventeenth and eighteenth centuries, and persisted into the nineteenth, were more a reversion to the pre-Reformation patterns of medieval scholasticism than a development of the Reformers' patterns. I am of course referring to preaching methodology, not subject matter! It is on the whole true to say that those who followed Calvin's style of continuous exposition, book by book, in the line of the ancient 'homily' were relatively few, and that they stand out in Scottish church history in the seventeenth to nineteenth centuries as largely untypical. It is only in the post-war years of the twentieth century that such preaching has begun to come into its own once again.

Reformation preaching

What was it which marked the Reformers' preaching as standing in marked contrast with that of medieval scholasticism, and indeed with much of what followed them from the seventeenth century onwards? Simply this: the Reformers went right back to scriptural patterns of preaching, to the 'homily', to the opening up and the unfolding of what the Scriptures said, giving the sense of it and causing people to understand the reading (Nehemiah 8:8) — in effect, a running commentary on Scripture, with application interspersed. This is what was so central to them, and it was a centrality that they found in the Scriptures themselves. No one can read

Scripture, and particularly the history of the early church, without being conscious of the paramount and indeed primary place that is given to preaching.

The enormous impact of the day of Pentecost in Acts 2 was made not by the mighty rushing wind and the cloven tongues as of fire, but by the proclamation of the Word. The spectacular manifestations, it is true, made the people ask 'What does this mean?'; but it was the preaching of the Word that pricked their hearts and made them say 'Men and brethren, what shall we do?'

When the work and witness of the church began to expand, and some of the implications of the Gospel began to become evident in the need for works of compassion and social concern, the apostles appointed deacons to supervise this, with the comment that 'It would not be right for us to neglect the ministry of the Word of God in order to wait on tables ... we will give our attention to prayer and the ministry of the Word' (Acts 6:2-4).

When persecution came, as it inevitably did, we are told that the early disciples, being scattered abroad, 'went everywhere preaching the Word' (Acts 8:4). The first great missionary outreach with the Gospel had its origins in Antioch in a church that was deeply taught in the Word.

The apostolic endeavour invariably took the form of a teaching ministry. They proved, as Paul makes clear at the outset of his first Corinthian epistle, that it pleased God by the foolishness of preaching to save those who believe.

It is in this context that we can best understand the comment made by Luke the historian about the extraordinary impact that the apostles' preaching had in Ephesus: 'So mightily grew the Word of God and prevailed' (Acts 19:20, AV).

The distinguished theologian of a former day, P.T. Forsyth, a graduate of Aberdeen University, makes this striking statement at the outset of his book, *Positive Preaching and the Modern Mind*: 'Preaching is the most distinctive institution of Christianity. With its preaching Christianity stands or falls'. In saying this he was simply reflecting the attitude and the conviction of the Reformers themselves, for they believed that it was the preaching of the Word of God which was the constituting essential of the ministry, and that all other duties attached to the minister's office are secondary to preaching. Before the administration of the sacraments, before the organisation and discipline, comes the preaching of the divine Word. The Reformers held that, when he was truly preaching the divine Word, the pastor was performing the most exalted work on earth. He was co-operating in the redemptive work of God, bringing sinners to salvation, building the church of Christ and, above all, glorifying God the Lord, whose ambassador he was.

Such was the conviction of the Reformers, and it was a conviction that was destined to revolutionize the whole of Europe in the fifteenth and sixteenth centuries. Beginning with Wyclif's Lollards, who travelled the length and breadth of England expounding the Scriptures and making known the message of the Gospel to the common people through the use of his translation of the Scriptures into English, it was truly 'an idea whose hour had come'. The movement gathered momentum and became literally irresistible, and the Reformation became a glorious fact — setting the whole of Europe aflame with its liberating message of grace.

The Reformation was indeed a return to, and a recovery of, the message of the Scriptures, and the preaching and exposition of that message in the way in which it was practised in the early church and in the first centuries of the Christian era. I noted earlier that all this makes certain definite assumptions about the nature of preaching itself, and flows from a certain doctrine of preaching. Two things require to be said about this. First, we must see the basic presuppositions underlying the essential need felt by the Reformers to make a clean break with existing forms and to turn to the New Testament model. Secondly, we must look at the Reformed doctrine of preaching itself.

A break with the past

As to the first of these, the Reformers resolutely believed and taught that the Scriptures were essentially intelligible to the ordinary spiritual mind. They refused to accept, as the Catholic Church had for so long taught, that it was too dangerous and difficult for ordinary folk to read and study Scripture for themselves — a belief that had made the Bible become a sealed book, of which there was a widespread and almost complete ignorance. For Calvin and his colleagues, the clamant need of that day and generation was for a knowledge of the Scriptures to be imparted to the common people. They had been denied it for so long, and now they were hungry for the Word of life. How else could that knowledge be imparted, except by the most comprehensive exposition of all its parts? As one Reformed writer was to put it, 'The analytic homily presents to the clergy an opportunity to aquaint both themselves and their audiences in a comparatively short time with the general content of Holy Writ' (R.B. Kuiper).

On the other hand — and this is even more basic and fundamental — the Reformers maintained that Christ and the Scriptures were inseparable, in the sense that it is only in and through the Scriptures that Christ can be known. Therefore, to communicate a whole Christ and mediate a whole salvation, a whole Bible is necessary; for Christ is in all the Scriptures, and everywhere, and in all its parts, a man hears 'His Master's Voice'. 'Study the Scriptures diligently', said our Lord, 'because you think that by them you possess eternal life. These are the Scriptures which testify about me' (John 5:39).

It can hardly be controverted that in respect to both these considerations, the wheel has come round full circle. Today, there is a widespread ignorance of the Scriptures throughout the land and, thankfully, a growing hunger in the hearts of men and women for the living Word. And there is a growing awareness of the need for a presentation of the message of the whole biblical revelation, with a view to the production of balanced and mature Christian character in the lives of God's people — the kind of character than can rejuvenate and regenerate society in our time.

The Reformed doctrine of preaching

We have already referred to the indissoluble bond that the Reformers regarded as existing between Christ and the Scriptures. This has significance for their doctrine of preaching, for the one is the corollary of the other. T.H.L. Parker, in his fine book on Calvin, *The Oracles of God*, discusses this at some length, and sums up the distinctive characteristics of the great Genevan Reformer's position:'Preaching is the Word of God, first, in the sense that it is an exposition and interpretation of the Bible, which is as much the Word of God as if men "heard the very words pronounced by God Himself".'

Preaching is the Word of God because the preacher has been sent and commissioned by God as his ambassador, the one who has authority to speak in his name.

Preaching is the Word of God in the sense that it is revelation. It is the Word of God when God speaks through the human words, revealing himself through them and using them as the vehicle of his grace. To use Calvin's own words: 'God deigns to consecrate the mouths and tongues of men to his service, making his own voice to be heard in them'. It is not so much that Calvin identifies the spoken, human word with the living Word of God — the distinction between the two is always there — but rather that he recognizes that God is pleased to speak in the word that is preached, as indeed is made clear in Acts 10:44: 'While Peter was still speaking these words, the Holy Spirit came on all who heard the message.'

Important implications

All this has practical and important implications. One is that it is the preaching, rather than the preacher, that is of decisive importance — the message rather than the messenger. This is of greater significance than is often realized. If the Gospel were, of course, simply a story to relate, then the important consideration would be the preacher: his style, his presentation, his oratory. But if the Gospel is, as the apostles and the Reformers held, the power of God unto salvation and not simply something attended by the power of God, then the emphasis necessarily passes from the preacher to the thing preached, and from the 'excellency of speech' and 'the enticing words of man's wisdom' — which Paul so explicitly and decisively abjured — to the message that comes 'in demonstration of the Spirit and of power'.

P.T. Forsyth is so right when he asserts that the Christian preacher is not the successor of the Greek orator but of the Hebrew prophet, with his 'Thus saith the

Lord'. Indeed, a very good case, and a compelling one, could be made for assert-ing that it was precisely the predominance of classical rhetoric and oratory, which in the early centuries were terms synonymous with higher education and were increasingly adopted by the leaders of the church, that ultimately obscured and all but destroyed the testimony of the church in the Middle Ages. This is why the Reformers so decisively repudiated it and returned to preaching as the exposition of Scripture, as in the patristic age, and established the tradition of continuous exposition of Scripture, preaching through the entire Bible, book by book.

One of the important implications in the assertion that the Scriptures are the liv-ing Word of God is that, when they are preached in the Spirit and understood by mind and heart, they exercise a dynamic influence upon life. This means that basi-cally, in our work for the Gospel, we must depend on the truth of God itself to do its own life-giving work, and trust in its power to do so. James Denney has a fine passage in one of his published sermons on our Lord's temptation. Speaking of Jesus' refusal to yield to the temptation to use methods which appeal rather to the senses than to the soul ('Throw yourself down from the pinnacle of the temple'), he goes on:

> How little he (Jesus) had of all that churches are tempted to trust in now! How little there is in the gospels about methods and apparatus! ... we may well believe he would look with more than amazement upon the importance which many of his disciples now attach to such things. 'He spake the word unto them', that was all. The trust of the church in other things is really a distrust of the truth, an unwillingness to believe that its power lies in itself, a desire to have something more irresistible than truth to plead truth's cause; all these are modes of atheism ... It is not only a mistake but a sin, to trust to attractions for the ear and the eyes, which are drawn to places of entertainment. What the evangelist calls 'the word' — the spiritual truth, the message of the Father and of his kingdom — spoken in the Spirit and enforced by the Spirit, told by faith and heard by faith — is our only real resource, and we must not be ashamed of its simplicity.

'Something more irresistible than truth to plead truth's cause'; is not this the condemnation of a great deal in Christian work today? Its failure is that men do not believe that the Word of God is a living Word. This is the need, and this is the way: subject the people to the Word of life, give the people the Scriptures, teach them, open them up, giving the understanding, and trust that the power of the Word will eventually ignite men's hearts, as it did here. This is the pattern. Do we really believe in the Word to that extent? Are we content to let the Word of God do this, in the faith and confidence that, in time, it will produce moral revolution and transformation? Or do we yield to the temptation, when nothing seems to hap-pen, to introduce other things to supplement this plain Bible teaching? Is this how we think in the secret of our hearts?

I suggest, with respect, that this has a great deal to say to the contemporary evangelical church and to the proliferation of parachurch organisations in their preoccupation and enthusiasm with things other than truth, where preaching is relegated to an increasingly minor and subordinate role and the singing of deplorable ditties has become the order of the day.

It seems to me that a false, defective and unbiblical concept of worship is at work here — as if worship could ever be divorced from the Word and the hearing of the Word. One of the purest expressions of worship in the Old Testament is found in Psalm 95: 'O come, let us worship and bow down ...' It is surely not without significance that almost in his next breath the psalmist says, 'Today if you will hear his voice, harden not your hearts'. This is the context in which biblical worship is set — the giving and hearing of the Word — and it is a dangerous deviation from the truth to imagine it is possible to have 'worship' or 'fellowship' apart from the Word.

Let me offer you a comment from a recent review of missionary interest in the student world:

> Christian Unions seem to spend more time in worship than they used to; whereas before you would have a short time of praise and then a forty-minute-plus Bible reading, it's now often the forty-minute-plus in worship and then a twenty-minute talk. An experiment carried out by a student group put a very dynamic personality into the Christian Union to give a very lighthearted talk full of very interesting stories. The following week they sent a more serious man who was a very good Bible teacher, and two or three weeks later they sent the students a questionnaire. Students all remembered the first speaker but could not remember very much from the second speaker at all. It seems that many students want the more lightweight talks now, which makes it doubly difficult for us to get over a biblical mission concern.

In my view, this is not a happy state of affairs to be obtaining in the student world at the present time; it is something very disquieting, and should be in the prayers of God's people.

The nature of expository preaching

The next point I want to make relates to the nature and rationale of expository ministry, and I would like to deal with this in two main parts.

Equipping the saints

The first of these is encapsulated in the apostle Paul's well known words in Ephesians 4, where he speaks of the institution by the exalted Christ of gifts of ministry in his church 'for the equipment of the saints for the service they are to render him, and for the edifying of the body of Christ' so as to bring them to maturity and stature in him. This is a magnificent passage, leading me to point out that there is a threefold ministry involved in the preaching of the Word.

Illumination for the ignorant

First of all, there is the illuminative aspect of ministry. Illumination is needed for the ignorant and the confused. This is a wide and important area for our consideration. We see it at work in the initial sense in the mystery of regeneration. It is the entrance of the divine word, as the psalmist says, that gives light. Faith comes by hearing, and hearing by the Word of God, and its first act is to open blinded eyes and minds to understand the truth of the Gospel. 'Do you understand what you are reading?' said Philip to the Ethiopian eunuch, and this was the beginning of things for him. And it is for us all.

But the illuminative act of the Word continues all along the line, for there are different kinds of ignorance and confusion for it to combat. It is safe to say that there is a great deal of ignorance in the minds and hearts of believers —perhaps especially young believers, but certainly not only those — concerning their position in Christ. This is very graphically and pointedly underlined by Paul in Romans 6, for example, in the repeated words 'Do you not know?' It is this ignorance of our position in Christ, of who we are, and what we are, and where we are, in him, that has led to a very great deal of confusion in the doctrine of sanctification, not to say impoverishment. This is why Paul writes as he does to the Ephesians (1:15 ff.), praying that the eyes of their understanding might be enlightened, that they may know the wealth of their position in Christ and the extent of their victory in him.

A very graphic illustration of the possibilities inherent in this idea of illumination is seen in the incident recorded in Acts 19, in which Paul encountered certain disciples in Ephesus whose experience was clearly defective. When asked about their knowledge and experience of the Holy Spirit, their rejoinder was, 'We have not even heard there is a Holy Spirit.' Ignorance was their problem. There were things which they needed to know, but which they did not know. And Paul's ministry to them was first of all, and necessarily, a ministry of illumination. They had to be made to understand some very necessary truths about the Spirit (19:4). I am aware, of course, of the controversial nature of this passage in Acts, but its precise interpretation need not concern us at this point. On any interpretation, these men entered into a fulness of experience they had never known before. They entered into their real heritage as children of God, and became men on fire for him — with what result we may see from the rest of the chapter! For their experience was the prologue and prelude to the tremendous and far-reaching impact on the whole city.

The words in Acts 19:20 (AV), 'So mightily grew the Word of God and prevailed' are an apt summary of what happened. In the space of three short years the name of Jesus was magnified in that heathen, idolatrous city, and the whole of

Asia heard the word of the Gospel. Is it not significant that the chapter which records this mighty work begins with a story which tells of how twelve disciples entered their real heritage and destiny as children of God? But we must not miss the import of these words quoted from 19:20: 'So mightily grew the Word ...' How can the Word grow? Well, it became bigger, greater, more majestic reality to these men. They discovered the wealth of the Gospel of grace. I do not think it could be overemphasized that this so often is the true nature of our impoverishment today. The first and crying need of our time is for a teaching ministry that will unfold to God's people the wealth of the Gospel of grace, so to open up the the the truths of salvation that their very greatness and majesty will overpower and overwhelm men. The need is for a teaching ministry that will kindle a great flame within, and that will consume the dross of lesser things in people into the kind of outreach that tells for the kingdom of God.

Therapy for the sick

Second, we have what can be called the therapeutic aspect of ministry. Light and illumination for the ignorant and confused is accompanied by therapy for the sick. If ignorance hinders development to spiritual maturity, so also does sickness in the spiritual life. In Ephesians 4:12, Paul uses a word translated in the AV as 'perfecting', which is full of significance in this connection. Its root meaning is 'to bring something or someone into its proper condition (whether for the first time or after a lapse)'. The word is used in classical Greek as a medical term for 'mending a broken joint', and appears in the New Testament in such contexts as 'mending torn nets' (Matt. 4:21) and 'restoring a backslider' (Gal. 6:1). These references are sufficient to indicate to us what may be called the 'therapy of the Word'. If a man's life is not what it should be, it is the therapeutic action of the Word that he needs. The Word will challenge him and convict, often on specific matters.

It is here that we see the true understanding of 'crisis' in spiritual experience. It is true that the illumination of the Word can bring sudden enlightenment: 'I see it now', we say, as the light floods in. That is a crisis, if you like, in our thinking. But with the therapeutic action of the Word, crisis can be very much more acute. 'If your right hand causes you to sin, cut it off and throw it away', says our Lord. That is crisis indeed, just as abdominal surgery is crisis surgery in the medical sphere. The diseased organ must be cut out if health is to be preserved.

But this surgery, it must be realized, is essentially a negative thing, and preparatory. It is not health itself; it simply removes that which makes good health impossible. So also, in spiritual life, the therapy of the Word does not in itself constitute growth and upbuilding; it simply makes growth possible by removing and dealing with things that have hitherto prevented it. Crisis, in the spiritual life, means just this, and we should not confuse it to mean that a man who has had a crisis-experience has 'arrived' in the spiritual sense, or is on a higher plane spiritually than others, any more than we can suppose that a man who has had major surgery is superior to those who have not. Indeed, a man who has undergone a spiritual crisis has only now begun. Real, meaningful Christian experience has only become possible now that hindrances to growth are out of the way. It is only because he has in fact fallen away from his first, original consecration that this crisis-therapy has become necessary. Something had gone wrong, that has now been put right.

This is where we can see real danger in what is sometimes called 'convention' ministry, if it makes the assumption, as it sometimes does, that everybody is sick and needs soul-surgery.

Food for the healthy

However, there is a third and very important aspect of ministry, namely its edifying and upbuilding function. There is illumination for the ignorant and confused, therapy for the sick, and now food for the healthy. When everything that hinders growth in the believer is removed — ignorance on the one hand, and disease on the other — he can then begin to grow to maturity, and in maturity, till he comes to the measure of the stature of the fulness of Christ.

Here it is the steady process of growth that is important — not an experience marked by crisis. Nor is there any short cut to such maturity — no simple, three-point plan that bypasses the serious business of Christian discipline, with its wrestling and battling and striving, with its daily obedience and daily dying to sin. Our Lord's parable of the seed growing secretly has relevance here: first the blade, then the ear, then the full corn in the ear. This is the pattern for positive Christian growth. Only by a steady submission to the discipline of the Word in all its fulness, as it ministers to us the riches of Christ and as it steadily and progressively masters us, do we develop the lineaments of character. For this, Christ has appointed ministers, prophets and teachers in the church, for the perfecting of the saints, to bring them to maturity in him.

For Paul, this meant the whole counsel of God. The fact is that we need all the truth of God for our balanced growth — not merely this or that doctrine, this or that emphasis. Christ is made unto us wisdom, righteousness, sanctification and redemption, and to get a whole Christ we need the whole Word. He is the life of the Word, and it all has sanctifying, edifying, upbuilding power. This is why undue emphasis on this or that 'theory' of sanctification, this or that preoccupation with a particular 'line' of interpretation, is often productive of confusion, not to say tension and stress, in Christian lives. And, I may say, there are far too many 'lines' being peddled today, all of them without exception claiming to be 'the answer'. Poor, anxious, distracted Christians go in their droves to find an ever-elusive answer (and sometimes at considerable financial cost and coming away disappointed), when all the time their real need could be met long-term by submitting themselves in earnest to the disciplines of the Word.

We need the whole counsel of God to make us what we ought to be. That is why there can never be any effective substitute for a fully and truly biblical ministry, whose range extends from Genesis to Revelation. And wherever you do have such a ministry, in which no concessions are made to carnal attitudes in Christians' hearts but, on the contrary, expository preaching is taken seriously, the results are always the same: not only does such a ministry produce fruit, but quality fruit. It builds men and women of calibre and character. God is faithful to his own Word.

A Presbyterian magazine in the United States tells of a minister who spent three months of sabbatical leave travelling around the country observing growing churches. In travelling 20,000 miles for this study,

> he found, among other things, that the preaching that God is using to help people is simply Bible teaching; it is not fancy oratory, not problem-centred, not filled with gimmicks. It is mainly a running commentary on the Scriptures, largely overlooking the homiletical tricks that must accompany the sermon that uses the Bible as a mere accessory ... These churches will not allow a twenty-minute sermon and theatrical productions to substitute for solid Bible teaching. Entire families come and enjoy long services. The confidence of preacher and people rests on the Word of God, allowing God to do his work through the Word ... The large attendances of some of these churches is accounted for...by the fact that people will come to a church where they are fed by the Word of God.

Engaging in expository ministry

The other aspect of the nature and rationale of expository ministry relates to the practical approach to it by those who engage in it. Let me say at the outset that it involves us in a great deal of disciplined study and basic spadework, in the exercise of 'rightly dividing the word of truth', as Paul puts it, and of being 'a workman that needeth not to be ashamed'.

Basic spadework

On the one hand, there is what I call the 'basic spadework' of getting down to and unearthing what the Scriptures say. The Reformers held to the truth that the meaning of the Word as it was originally given, is the meaning that bears the message of God to the people. That often needs a great deal of excavation, a great deal of study, with the help of all possible aid from the scholars and commentators. I have often urged the students in my congregation to 'major' on commentaries, expository and exegetical rather than devotional, in their buying of theological books. If the centrally important thing is what the Scriptures are saying, then it is our duty to get down to that first of all, and most of all.

That being said, however, we have to add two other considerations. One is that the details of historical introduction, time and place of writing, and so on, are not meant to be the substance of our preaching. True, there are a great many scholarly issues and problems involved in, say, the study of a gospel, but this is not the substance of preaching. Even if it were, you can get all of it in any good Bible dictionary or handbook. And I do not see it as the preacher's task to give in the pulpit what people can get from the dictionaries. James Denney has some trenchant things to say in this regard. Commenting on Paul's words in 2 Corinthians 1:19,20, he says:

> The Gospel, which is identified with God's Son, Jesus Christ, is here described as a mighty affirmation. It is not Yes and No, a message full of inconsistencies, or ambiguities, a proclamation the sense of which no one can ever be sure he has grasped. In it (*en auto* means 'in Christ') the everlasting Yea has found place. The perfect tense (*gegonen*) means that this grand affirmation has come to us, and is with us, for good and all. What it was and continued to be in Paul's time, it is to this day. It is in this positive, definite, unmistakable character that the strength of the Gospel lies. What a man cannot know, cannot seize, cannot tell, he cannot preach. The refutation of popular errors, theories, even about Scriptures, is not Gospel; the intellectual 'economy', with which a clever man in a dubious position uses language about the Bible or its doctrines which to the simple means Yes, and to the subtle qualifies the Yes enormously, is not Gospel. There is no strength in any of these things. Dealing in them does not make character simple, sincere, massive, Christian. When they stamp themselves on the soul, the result is not one to which we could make the appeal Paul makes here. If we have any Gospel at all, it is because there are things which stand for us above all doubts, truths so sure that we cannot question them, so absolute that we cannot qualify them, so much our life that to tamper with them is to touch our very heart. Nobody has any right to preach who has not mighty affirmations to make concerning God's Son, Jesus Christ — affirmations in which there is no ambiguity, and which no questioning can reach.

By the same token, thorough and disciplined study with commentaries does not mean that it is a question of relating and passing on in preaching what we have read in the commentaries. Rather, our preaching is meant to be a living Word, a Word from God, that precisely you do not get from commentaries. This never means that we should not bother to read them. Indeed we should! It is when the spadework is done, or being done, that the study and discipline involved act as a kind of catalyst, and from the study there emerges the authentic Word from the Lord. This comes from the study and hard spadework, and is not there without it. Sir Thomas Taylor, former Principal of Aberdeen University, and devout believer, used to say, 'The Scriptures do not yield their treasures to chance enquiry'.

Therefore, expository preaching is never merely exposition and exegesis, but these and something else: the ministry of the Holy Spirit of God, who alone can make it into food for the soul, for building up men in the faith — spiritual nurture, as an answer to the prayer 'Give us this day our daily bread'. We cannot, when men ask us for bread, be content to give them a stone.

For my own part, over the years, and increasingly as the years pass, I have found the need to dig ever more deeply into the Scriptures, and to lay the learning of the church down the ages under tribute as much as it is in my power to do so. Demanding as it undoubtedly is, it more and more brings a resilience of mind and spirit, and a sense of buoyancy to preaching.

But, you may say, 'The time all this must take!' Yes, indeed, but it is a question of priorities, is it not? Let me remind you of Paul's exhortation to Timothy, 'Preach the word; be prepared in season, out of season' (2 Tim 4:1-5).

No one can mistake the urgency in Paul's words as he bids the young Timothy 'preach the Word', and this serves to remind us that time is not on our side in our concern to build and establish a bulwark of this nature against the surging tides of lawlessness and anarchism in our day. There is a crying need for the church to recover its faith in the divine Word it has been commissioned to preach, to recover also its faith in preaching as the God-appointed means of communicating the divine power to human situations that desperately need it. It is clear to me that since this is the weapon above all others which is mighty through God to the pulling down of strongholds, the preaching of the Word should be the church's paramount and urgent priority. It is plain that even in the context of the conscious needs of the time, this is not always the case; plain also that this urgent priority very readily tends to become submerged in a multitude of 'other things' — many of them worthy and good, some less so, but all alike deadly dangerous in the time and attention they succeed in filching from 'the one thing needful'. All else in the life of the church should be subservient to the labour of preaching and its necessary adjunct of spiritual counselling and pastoral work. We in the ministry must make it our business to see to it that whatever else suffers in the busy round of our work (and there will always be more do do than can be done by one man), the time that requires to be given to preparation of heart and mind for the pulpit will not suffer but be kept sacrosanct. And God's people too, if they are wise, will see to it that their demands on their ministers will not be such that they make this a practical impossibility for them. For, unless they do, they will find that the practical effectiveness and fruitfulness of their work will become subject to the law of diminishing returns, and a pattern will emerge in which more and more activity will produce less and less spiritual vitality and fruit, until a point is reached when the true work of the Gospel is relegated to a relatively, if not completely, insignificant place.

A people of prayer

This is something which wise and discerning Christians can do a great deal to bring about. There is a great need for a praying people to get behind those called and ordained to preach the Word, and by the very force and intensity of their prayers to thrust them out into a truly powerful and prophetic ministry that will disturb the national conscience and bring about upheaval in contemporary society in a way that has been known in the past history of our land. It is ours to demand of God that this will be the kind of ministry he will give to his church in our time. Let it not be thought that this is asking for the impossible. Think of the Reformation in Scotland. When God gave back his Word to the people, through the ministry of Knox and his colleagues, in a comparatively short time a moral and spiritual transformation became a fact throughout the whole nation. It could happen again. It needs to happen again. If it does not happen again, the outlook for the future is very bleak indeed.

Authority in preaching

Perhaps it is necessary to be more specific, however, in defining what we mean by the recovery of the Word. It is not so much the Word itself that needs to be recovered, for indeed, in the mercy of God, we have not been without the Word in our land for a very long time. There is still the open Book and freedom to read it. But what we do lack, and have lacked, is the Word spoken and proclaimed with authority. You will recall that what startled the people in our Lord's day was not so much the content of his teaching, although it was of course deeply impressive, as the fact that he spoke with authority and not as the scribes. What we are in such sore need of today is that the blessed Gospel of Christ should be proclaimed with a divine authority that is manifest and unmistakeable and that will not only oblige men to hear it but also make a telling impact on society. Nor is this to be construed as preaching the word of salvation merely in evangelistic terms — although of course this is included — for this is not really what Paul means by the words 'do the work of an evangelist'. Lock, in ICC renders it, 'Do the work of one who has a Gospel to preach'. And the Gospel we have to preach is the whole counsel of God. If all Scripture is given by inspiration of God and is profitable, then all of it, not merely some of it, must be preached, if a whole Christ, and therefore a whole salvation, is to be communicated to men and women. Nothing less than this can be said to be fulfilling the calling, and doing the work, of an evangelist, of one who has a Gospel to preach.

Not that such a task will ever be easy and, significantly, Paul reminds Timothy of the afflictions it would involve for him. His argument runs like this: Watch! Let nothing deflect you from the centrality of the Gospel. Keep near its heart, which is the Cross. Remember that all the enemy's wiles are directed towards one objective in the Christian's life — to get him away from the Cross. But stand firm, whatever afflictions may come to you. And come they will, for it will cost you to keep near the Cross, both outwardly and inwardly. You will lose your popularity with worldly believers if you stab their consciences with your faithful words, and they will slight you, despise you, and heap reproaches on you. That will be part of your outward affliction. And Satan will not be slow to stir up inward corruption either. The Cross-life will mean many a lonely wrestling. But hold fast, Timothy; even if it breaks you, no matter, for your name will be Israel, and you will be a prince with God.

Recovery of the Word in this sense is what we need: in the sense of a ministry that is going to make no concessions to the worldly-wise or the half-hearted, that refuses to 'come down' to making an appeal to itching ears, catering for carnal Christian palates, providing a soul-destroying substitute for the death men have refused to die — for this is what accounts for the decline in our evangelical testimony from the integrity of true and honourable exposition of the Word.

But to return to the matter of the recovery of authority once again: What is it that constitutes this authority? It is certainly true that we need a widespread return to the faith once for all delivered to the saints. We are hardly likely to find a biblical authority in a non-biblical or antibiblical ministry. But orthodoxy can be dead as well as living, whether orthodoxy of doctrine or church order. And it is the undoubted verdict of history, if not our own, that impeccable orthodoxy does not of itself guarantee the unction of the Spirit of God nor his anointing on the preaching of the word of salvation. Indeed, there is an orthodoxy which can on occasion make the glorious truths of the Gospel sound dull and dreary.

Seeking the blessing of God

Paul speaks in 1 Thessalonians 1:5 of preaching 'not simply with words, but also with power, with the Holy Spirit and with deep conviction.' Paul had that unction, and knew that he had it. He speaks of what manner of men he and his companions had been among the Thessalonians. They were men who magnified the Saviour, in lives that were well saved, wrought upon in the deep places by the healing and sanctifying Spirit. They were, as he says in 1 Thessalonians 2:4, 'tried out for God, then trusted for service' — put to the test and trusted for service.

Let me give you some Scriptures to underline this thought and principle. 'Jesus did not commit himself unto them...for he knew what was in man'(John 2:24). This is paralleled in the experience of the ministry. The blessing of God, and the unction of the Spirit are not easily won!'The Holy Spirit was not yet given, because Jesus was not yet glorified' (John 7:37 ff.). It is true that every believer has the Spirit, but God's seal on our testimony comes only when Christ is glorified in heart and life. In the experience of the ministry and in personal witness alike, coronation precedes Pentecost. Look at 2 Corinthians 4 — we say, 'Christ lives in me'. Yes, but he needs to get through us. And for this, we must be 'get-through-able'. This is what Paul is getting at when he speaks of the treasure of Gospel-light in earthen vessels. Matthew Henry suggests that the story of Gideon and the 300 may be in Paul's mind here. The earthen pitchers had to be shattered to let the lights shine out against the enemy. Paul speaks of how he bears about in his body the dying of the Lord Jesus, that the life also of Jesus might be manifest in him. The vessel has to be broken to let the light out to men. Death works!

Now, this is simply an expression, an extension, of the principle Paul elsewhere unfolds in 1 Corinthians 1, when he speaks of God choosing the weak things of the world to confound the things that are mighty. 'Weakness' gives him the opportunity and 'lets him through', so to speak, to the world he longs to bless and save. It was the 'weakness' of Christ's utter submission to and dependence on God that enabled God to establish the bridgehead of grace in the world, and the principle applies also to all who will serve him. The 'weakness' of the believer's crucifixion, the breaking of the vessel which is his life, is the way God gets through to men, the channel by which blessing comes. This is the explanation of such passages as 1 Corinthians 4:9-13, 'It seems to me that God has put us apostles on display at the end of the procession...condemned to die...', and 1 Corinthians 2:2-4, 'in weakness, fear and much trembling...'. One of the Hudson Taylor family has said, 'Blood of our own must attest our faith in the precious blood of Christ if we would share and show forth the victory of the cross'.

'In deaths oft' — this is the pattern for the pulpit, for all who would proclaim the saving word of Christ. The word 'blessing' is said to come from an old Anglo-Saxon word meaning 'blood'. In this warfare, only the wounded can serve. Witness and preaching are effective only when there is a 'cross' at the heart of Christian experience.

There is a wonderful testimony given to the worth of John the Baptist's ministry by those who heard him: 'Though John never performed miraculous signs, all that John said about this man (Jesus) was true' (John 10:41) — not the spectacular, not the sensational, but a faithful witness to Christ! To speak true things truly about Christ, from hearts that God has touched, with lips touched with holy fire, and under the constraint of divine love, is the great and crying need of our time. That is my dream, that more and more there will be those who will catch the vision. Our day and generation has yet to see what God can do with such a band of men.

He which hath no stomach to this fight,
Let him depart...
But we in it shall be remembered;
We few, we happy few, we band of brothers;
For he today that sheds his blood with me
Shall be my brother.

(Shakespeare, Henry V. IV.iii.35)

The Revd **James Philip** became minister of Holyrood Abbey Church of Scotland, Edinburgh, in 1958 and is widely known for his preaching and writing ministry. The text of this booklet was first presented to an audience in St George's Tron Church, Glasgow.

ORTHOS

Fellowship of Word and Spirit is a registered charity, no. 293159